The Solar System

Melvin and Gilda Berger

SCHOLASTIC INC.
New York Toronto London Auckland Sydney
Mexico City New Delhi Hong Kong Buenos Aires

Photographs: Cover: V.C.L./Taxi/Getty Images;
p. 1: Detlev van Ravenswaay/Photo Researchers, Inc.; p. 3: V.C.L./Taxi/Getty Images;
p. 4: David A. Hardy/Photo Researchers, Inc.;
p. 5: Antonio M. Rosario/The Image Bank/Getty Images;
p. 6: Mehau Kulyk/Photo Researchers, Inc.;
p. 7: Chris Hackett/The Image Bank/Getty Images; p. 8: Vincent Di Fate;
p. 9: Science Photo Library;
p. 10: NASA/Dembinsky Photo Assoc.; p. 11: Digital Vision/Getty Images;
p. 12: John Sanford/Photo Researchers, Inc.; p. 13: Gordon Garradd/Photo Researchers, Inc.;
p. 14: Adastra/Taxi/Getty Images; p. 15: Astrofoto/Shigemi Numazawa/Peter Arnold, Inc.;
p. 16: Antonio M. Rosario/The Image Bank/Getty Images.

The paintings in this book are artists' representations of the planets and do not always show the rings around Jupiter, Uranus, and Neptune. The rings around Saturn are always shown.

Photo Research: Sarah Longacre

ISBN 0-439-57474-9

12 11 10   6 7 8 9/0
                                                                                                        08

Printed in the U.S.A.
First printing, January 2004

The solar system is a family.

The solar system has many parts.

The sun is at the center.

Nine planets go around the sun.

Earth is one of the nine planets.

Fun Fact
Earth has one moon.

Seven planets have
one moon or more.

The moons go around the planets.

Asteroids are big rocks.

Asteroids go around the sun.

Comets are balls of ice.

Comets go around the sun.

Fun Fact
Shooting stars is another name for meteors (MEE-tee-orz).

Shooting stars are bits of rock or iron that fall to Earth.

Bits of rock or iron
go around the sun.

The solar system is
a great BIG family!